Rocks

Emily Ballinger

I like to collect rocks.
I look for different kinds of rocks.

3

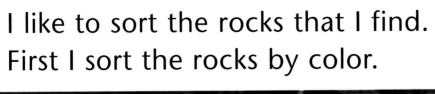

I like to sort the rocks that I find.
First I sort the rocks by color.

4

How many rocks are in each group?

gray

brown

white

mixed

7

Next I sort the rocks a different way.
I put smooth rocks in one group.
I put rough rocks in another group.

Which of these groups
has more rocks?

smooth

rough

11

I sort the smooth rocks by color.
I sort the rough rocks by color too.

13

How many rocks are smooth
and gray?
How many rocks are rough
and brown?

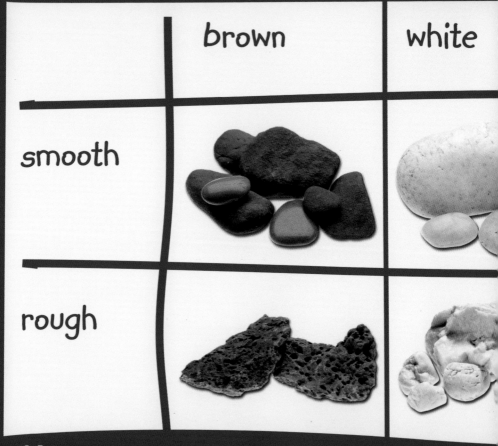

	brown	white
smooth		
rough		

gray

mixed
colors

Is there another way to sort
the rocks?